T0195602

LOGIC SAFARI

SAFARI

Book 2 · Grades 3-4

Written by Bonnie Risby

Illustrated by Annelise Palouda

First published in 2005 by Prufrock Press Inc.

Published in 2021 by Routledge
605 Third Avenue, New York, NY 10017
2 Park Square, Milton Park, Abingdon, Oxon OX14 4RN

Routledge is an imprint of the Taylor & Francis Group, an informa business.

ISBN: 9781593630904 (pbk)

DOI: 10.4324/9781003236290

Contents

Information for the Instructor

Pack your gear and get ready to take your students on a safari. But on this safari, you won't be stalking wild animals. You'll be stalking clues that you can piece together to solve deductive logic puzzles. The reward for this expedition will be a bounty of thinking skills. *Logic Safari* gives students an opportunity to sort through related bits of information by combining, relating, ordering, and eliminating. The result is the logical linking together of ideas that leads to the puzzle's solution.

Each puzzle in *Logic Safari* has three parts. These parts are:
1. **The introduction** - This paragraph sets the background and helps students become familiar with the elements of the puzzle.
2. **The clues** - The clues relate all of the components and provide a basis for the logical linking together of the pieces of information, thereby allowing students to make deductions that will lead to the solution.
3. **The grid** - The grid provides a worksheet for sorting, eliminating and associating the clues. Every square on the grid represents a possible answer. By eliminating possibilities, one is finally left with only one choice per row or column. The one square that is not been eliminated is one correct solution. When this is done for every row and column, the puzzle solution is complete.

Any marking system for the grid is valid if it is used consistently. Many students prefer to use an **X** in a square to represent elimination of a choice and an **O** to represent a correct answer. Using "yes" and "no" works equally well.

In addition to these three parts, students may wish to jot down notes on scratch paper. This may help them in putting the information in rank order or in visualizing the relationships. It should be stressed that there is always more than one way to correctly solve a puzzle; and in sharing the way in which each person used the clues to arrive at the solution, students will gain insights into different modes of thinking.

Students will find that it is necessary to look not only at each clue individually, but also to look at the clues in relation to one another in order to derive as much information as possible. For example, if the clues state, "Gina is older than Eric and the girl with the teddy bear but younger than Gonzales," we can deduce a lot of information by the proper arrangement of the clues. If there four people in the puzzle, we know that Gina is second in rank of age. If there are two boys and two girls, we also know that Gonzales is a boy. We can also deduce that Mary is not Gonzales, Eric is not Gonzales, Gonzales does not have a teddy bear, Gina does not have a teddy bear, and Eric does not have a teddy bear. In addition, we know that Gonzales is the oldest. With one clue, then we have been able to make several eliminations and two positive connections.

There are three books in this series, so students are able to move from easy to intermediate levels of difficulty in deductive thinking. *Logic Safari* puzzles are an excellent way to strengthen students' logical deductive thinking skills. Students find the puzzles very motivating, and as they work with these puzzles they grow in their abilities to sort through information and make connections.

Fantastic Gymnastics

Erin, Julie, Megan and Angela are all in the same gymnastics class. Their instructor puts each girl at a different station to work on the balance beam, vault, trampoline and parallel bars. Flip through these clues to discover which girl is working on each kind of equipment.

Clues

1. Erin and her friend who is on the balance beam are more advanced than Julie.

2. Megan and her friend who is on the trampoline are better at round-offs than Angela and Julie.

3. The girl practicing on the vault and Julie both hope to do well in the up coming competition.

4. The instructor did not send Megan to the balance beam.

	balance beam	vault	trampoline	parallel bars
Erin				
Julie				
Megan				
Angela				

© Taylor & Francis Group · *Logic Safari, Book 2* **DOI: 10.4324/9781003236290-1**

Cafeteria Choices

Lollie, Jay, Dominick and Kristi got in line at the cafeteria at the same time. Each one chose a different lunch. The lunches they chose were a slice of pizza, a taco, a sloppy Joe and a hot dog. Eat through the clues to discover what each student chose for lunch.

Clues

1. Jay is in the same class as the girl who chose a sloppy Joe and the girl who picked the hot dog.

2. Dominick told the others that he was allergic to pizza.

3. Lollie hates hot dogs.

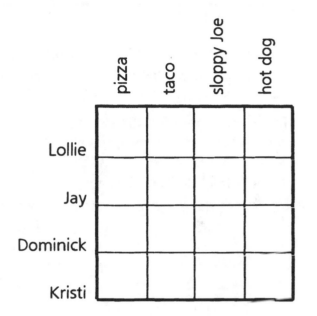

	pizza	taco	sloppy Joe	hot dog
Lollie				
Jay				
Dominick				
Kristi				

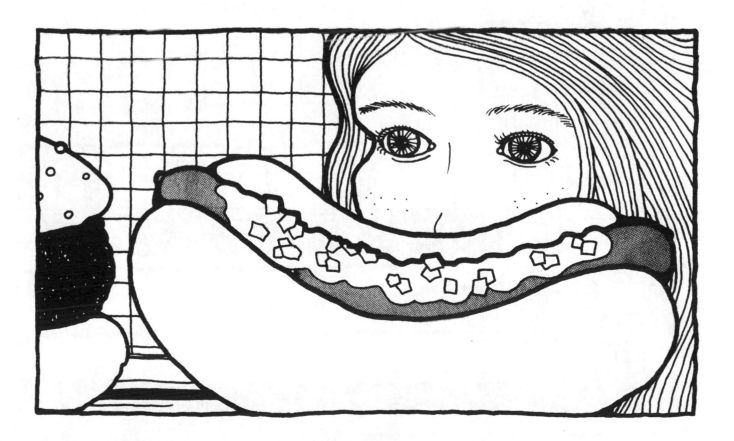

Special Delivery

Sarah, Jonathan and Kristina are students in Mrs. Heath's class. They ride to and from school on buses 54, 86 and 112. These buses are driven by Mr. Cipponeri, Ms. Walker and Mr. Dye. Steer your way through these clues to find which bus each student rides and who drives each bus.

Clues

1. Sarah, and the boy who takes Ms. Walker's bus, and the girl traveling on bus 54, all arrive between 8:10 and 8:15.

2. Mr. Cipponeri, who dressed up as a doctor on Halloween, gave Kristina a tiny candy bar as she got off his bus that afternoon.

3. Mr. Dye drives bus 86.

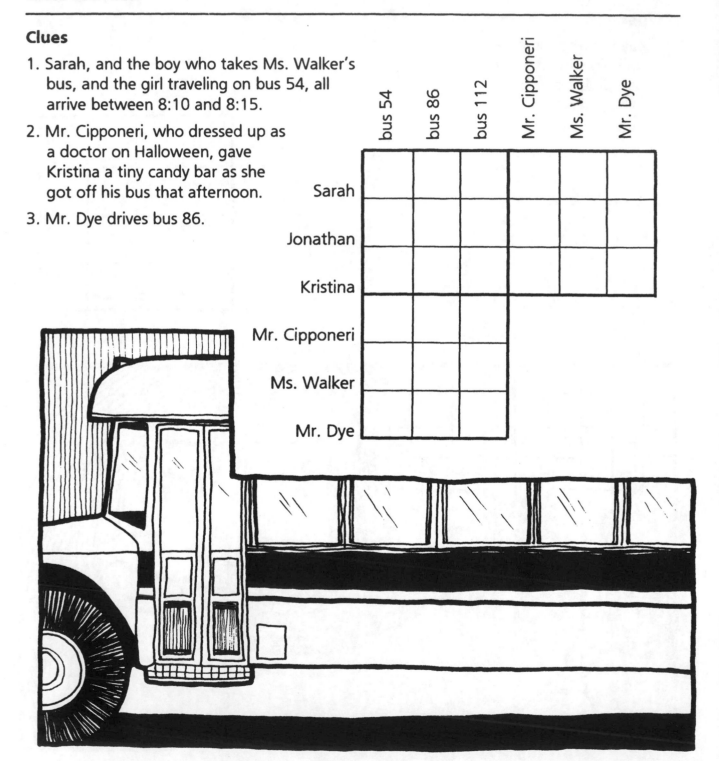

© Taylor & Francis Group • *Logic Safari, Book 2*   DOI: 10.4324/9781003236290-3

Lost and Found

After morning announcements Mrs. DuPont asked the students to check the lost and found box during their breaks. Michelle, Jason and Benjamin were looking for a purple mitten, a ski hat and a wind breaker. Sort through the clues to determine who found what missing item and when.

Clues

1. Jason and Benjamin went to the lost and found as soon as they finished lunch and retrieved a ski hat and a missing purple mitten.

2. Jason has never owned a pair of purple mittens.

	morning break	lunch break	lunch break	purple mitten	ski hat	windbreaker
Michelle						
Jason						
Benjamin						

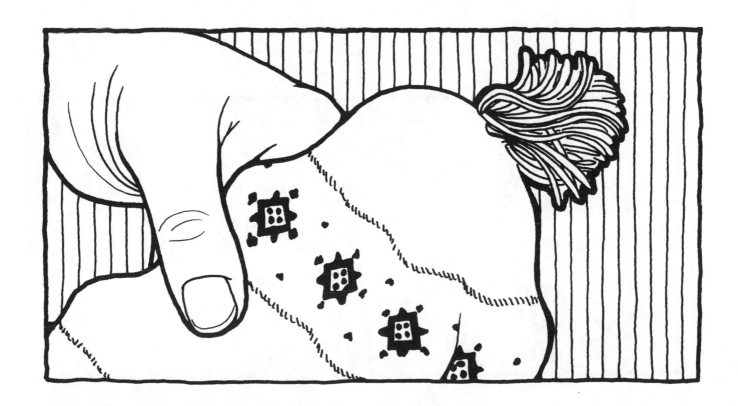

Bookmark Designers

Miss Roe, the librarian, held a contest for students to design bookmarks that would be given to anyone checking out a library book. Shannon, Laura and Robert had winning designs. Their bookmarks featured a rainbow of books, a pyramid of authors and a garden of blooming books. Miss Roe had them printed on gold, green and pink paper. Check out the clues to find out which student designed which bookmark.

Clues

1. The girl who designed the rainbow bookmark and the girl whose bookmark was printed on gold paper both stay for the after-school play program.

2. The pyramid bookmark was printed on gold paper.

3. Laura did not design the rainbow.

4. Robert's bookmark was not printed on pink paper.

	rainbow	pyramid	garden	gold	green	pink
Shannon						
Laura						
Robert						
gold						
green						
pink						

© Taylor & Francis Group • *Logic Safari, Book 2*   DOI: 10.4324/9781003236290-5

Coat Hooks

David, Melinda and Cole are second graders in Ms. Goodman's, Ms. Heath's and Ms. Meyers' classes. They are assigned coat hooks numbered 8, 14 and 16. Hook your way through the clues to discover which student is assigned which coat hook in the hallway.

Clues

1. David and the boy in Ms. Goodman's class have only one coat hook separating their hooks.

2. The girl in Ms. Meyers' class often leaves her book bag in the hallway.

3. Ms. Heath's student is assigned to hook number 16.

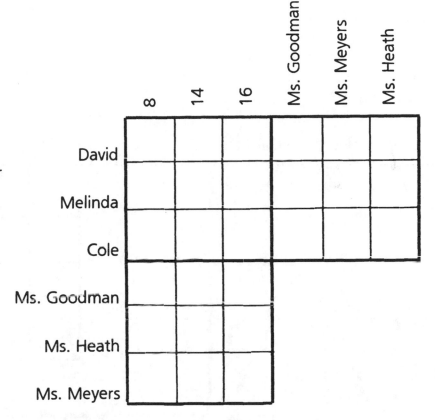

DOI: 10.4324/9781003236290-6 © Taylor & Francis Group • *Logic Safari, Book 2*   **9**

Fitness Profile

Mrs. Parker and Mr. Duke are making a fitness profile of all of their students. Their data shows that Grant, Mary and Garrett have the highest scores for either the one-mile run, pull-ups, or sit-ups. The students are 6, 7 and 9 years old. Sprint through these clues to find out the students' ages and in what activity they excel.

Clues

1. The girl who excels in sit-ups, the boy who is 6 years old, and the boy who excels at the one-mile run are all good sports whether they win or lose.

2. Mary is older than Garrett but younger than the boy who excels at the one-mile run.

	one-mile run	pull-ups	sit-ups	6 years	7 years	9 years
Grant						
Mary						
Garrett						
6 years						
7 years						
9 years						

Class Trip

Mr. Varga's class was planning a trip. The zoo, the museum and the art center were suggested by Kelly, Adam and Andrea. In the final vote the destinations received 6, 6 and 9 votes. Tally the clues and determine who suggested which destination and how many votes each place received.

Clues

1. The girl who suggested the museum received the same number of votes as the boy who suggested the zoo.

2. Andrea's suggestion was the most popular.

	zoo	museum	art center	6	6	9
Kelly						
Adam						
Andrea						
6			
6			
9			

Favorite Sports

Three of the favorite sports in Mr. Driskill's class are football, swimming and baseball. In Mr. Driskill's survey of favorite sports, each sport received either 10, 6 or 3 votes. Drew, Mark and Emily each voted for their favorite sport. Tackle the clue and find out whose favorite sport received the most votes.

Clues

1. Drew's sport received more votes than the girl whose favorite sport is swimming but fewer votes than baseball.

	football	swimming	baseball	10	6	3
Drew						
Mark						
Emily						
10			
6			
3			

© Taylor & Francis Group • *Logic Safari, Book 2*   DOI: 10.4324/9781003236290-9

Piggy Banks

Three friends (Marie, Vanessa and Katie) got new piggy banks. Each one put in a different number of coins in her bank that equaled a different value. Total up the clues to discover how much money each girl put in her piggy bank.

Clues

1. Marie put in more coins than the girl depositing 75 cents but fewer coins than Katie.

2. Marie put in more money than the girl with 5 coins but less money than the girl with 3 coins.

	75 cents	45 cents	33 cents	3 coins	4 coins	5 coins
Marie						
Vanessa						
Katie						
3 coins						
4 coins						
5 coins						

Cans for Conservation

The mobile recycling center is coming to school so that students can recycle their crushed cans. Margaret, Bradley and Tyler are in different grades and will deposit their cans at different times. Recycle these clues to determine each student's grade and at which time each will go to the recycling center.

Clues

1. Margaret, the boy in fifth grade, and the boy who will go to the trailer at 9:15 are all helping their school earn money to be used for a nature trail.

2. Bradley will deposit his cans before the kindergarten student and after the boy in fifth grade.

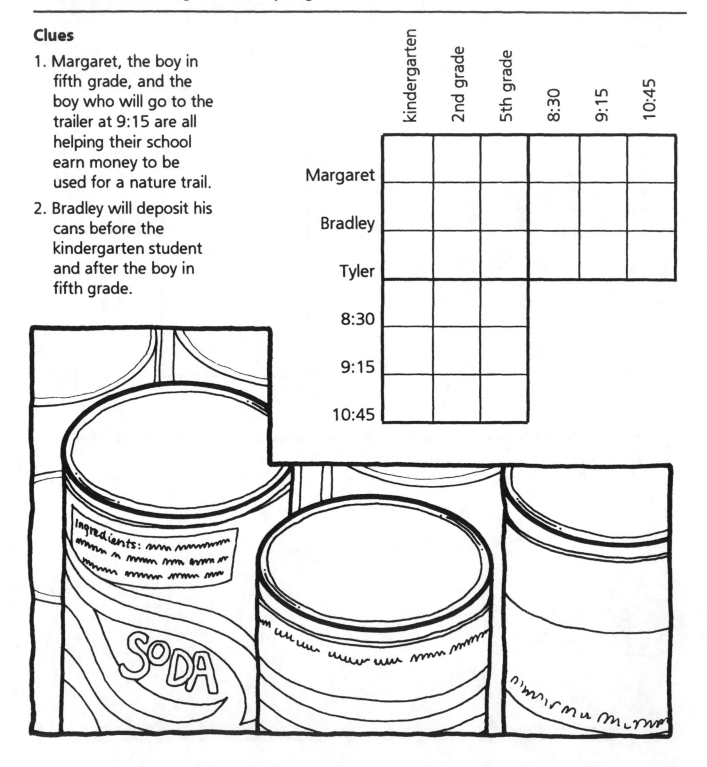

© Taylor & Francis Group • Logic Safari, Book 2   DOI: 10.4324/9781003236290-11

Class Quilt

Mrs. Byrd's class is making quilt blocks for a class quilt. Tommy, Catherine and Pamela are designing blocks that feature a pine tree, the Big Dipper and musical notes. They are planning to use embroidery, fabric paints and applique to fashion their blocks. Stitch up these clues to discover who is making each design and what technique they will use.

Clues

1. Tommy has trouble handling needles so his pine tree will not be stitched or embroidered.

2. Catherine has designed a block to highlight her talents of embroidery and playing the clarinet.

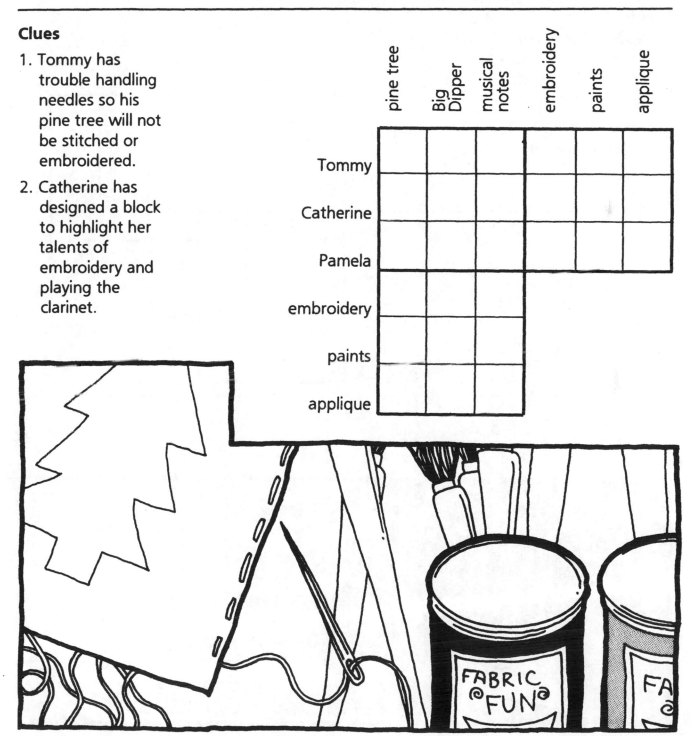

Student Council

Heather, Greg and Kevin were recently elected to the student council offices of president, secretary and historian. They are in the fourth, fifth and sixth grades. Consult the clues to determine who holds each office and what grade they are in.

Clues

1. Heather is in a lower grade than the boy who is president and the boy who is historian.

2. Greg is in a higher grade than the historian.

	president	secretary	historian	4th grade	5th grade	6th grade
Heather						
Greg						
Kevin						
4th grade						
5th grade						
6th grade						

© Taylor & Francis Group · Logic Safari, Book 2   DOI: 10.4324/9781003236290-13

Wind Chimes

Mr. Harris' class constructed unusual wind chimes for an art project. Suzanne, Janet and Candy made their chimes from nails, sea shells and antique spoons. They strung them from a piece of driftwood, a plastic lid and a cedar dowel. Untangle these clues to discover how each student's chimes were constructed.

Clues

1. Suzanne, and the girl using sea shells, and the girl using a cedar dowel came up with their designs all by themselves.

2. The girl who used nails for the chimes, the girl with the plastic lid for a hanger, and Candy used nylon filament to string their chimes to their hangers.

3. Janet used a large plastic lid as a hanger for her chimes.

	nails	sea shells	antique spoons	driftwood	plastic lid	cedar dowel
Suzanne						
Janet						
Candy						
driftwood						
plastic lid						
cedar dowel						

Bookmobile

Jack, Kimberly and Phillip are three second graders who visit the bookmobile each week. Their visits are scheduled for Tuesday morning, Tuesday afternoon and Wednesday morning. They are in rooms 2a, 2b and 2c. Check out the clues to find out the students' classrooms and when they visit the bookmobile.

Clues

1. Jack, and the second grader who visits the bookmobile on Tuesday afternoon, and the boy in 2b all look forward to choosing books at the bookmobile.

2. The student in 2c visits the bookmobile before the student in 2b but after the student in 2a.

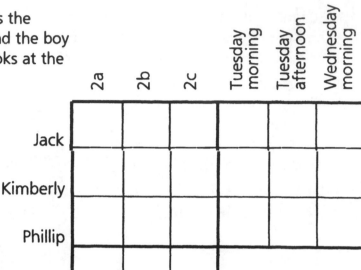

	2a	2b	2c	Tuesday morning	Tuesday afternoon	Wednesday morning
Jack						
Kimberly						
Phillip						
Tuesday morning						
Tuesday afternoon						
Wednesday morning						

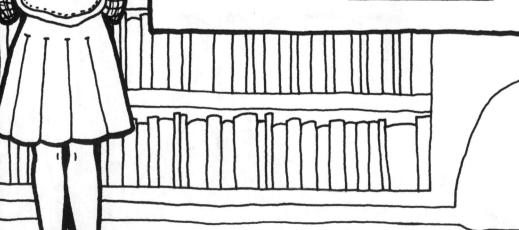

© Taylor & Francis Group • *Logic Safari, Book 2*   DOI: 10.4324/9781003236290-15

Baby-sitting

Mike is having three baby-sitters in the near future. The sitters are Kristen, Dara and Chad. They are scheduled to baby-sit on a Saturday afternoon, a Friday evening and a Wednesday after school. Mike's parents will be at a business meeting, enjoying a hockey game and celebrating their friends' anniversary. Sort through the clues and match the correct sitter with the correct day and activity.

Clues

1. Kristen, the boy who will sit on Saturday, and the girl sitting during the hockey game all live within walking distance of Mike's home.

2. Mike's parents have tickets for the hockey game on Friday.

3. The anniversary party is on a Saturday evening.

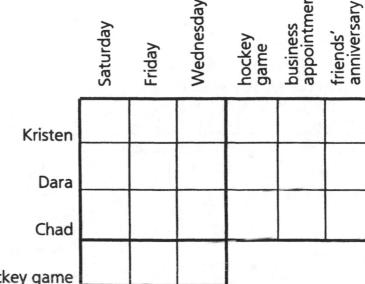

Turtle Race

Four boys raced their pet turtles named Tiny Tim, Tweedledum, Pokey and Ferdinand. They used their pets' favorite foods (strawberries, lettuce, cantaloupe and pickled beets) to lure them toward the finish line. Race through these clues to discover which food each turtle craved and in what order they finished the race.

Clues

1. Tweedledum finished before the turtle who loves lettuce and the turtle who yearns for cantaloupe, but after Tiny Tim.

2. Pokey finished after the turtle who loves strawberries and the turtle with a taste for pickled beets, but before the turtle who prefers cantaloupe.

3. Tweedledum does not like strawberries.

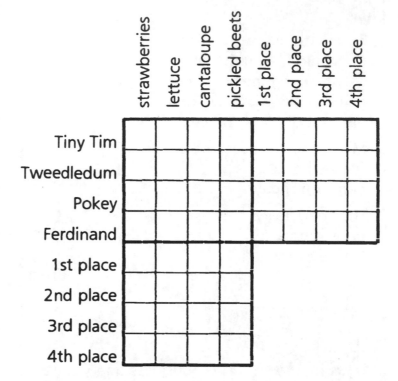

	strawberries	lettuce	cantaloupe	pickled beets	1st place	2nd place	3rd place	4th place
Tiny Tim								
Tweedledum								
Pokey								
Ferdinand								
1st place				
2nd place				
3rd place				
4th place				

     © Taylor & Francis Group • *Logic Safari, Book 2*   **DOI: 10.4324/9781003236290-17**

Cloud Mirages

Brittany, Tricia, Raymond and Samantha had a picnic. Afterwards they relaxed in the meadow by watching the clouds and comparing the images they saw. The shapes they pointed out to each other were a sad lady, a winged horse, a soldier and a sailing ship. Each said cloud gazing gave them a certain feeling. The clouds made them feel peaceful, content, curious or sad. Float through these clues to determine who saw what and how they felt while watching the clouds.

Clues

1. Britanny, the boy who sighted a soldier, the girl who saw the sad lady's face, and the girl who said she felt peaceful while watching the clouds were amazed at the images their friends saw in the same clouds.

2. Tricia, the boy who felt content, the girl who saw a winged horse, and the girl who felt curious all enjoyed the picnic in the meadow.

3. Brittany, Raymond, Samantha, and the girl who felt sad are close friends.

4. The person who observed the winged horse did not feel sad.

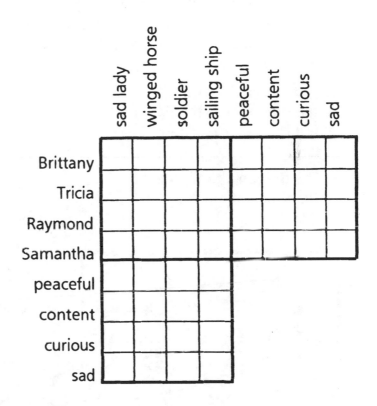

Kites

Seth, Louise, Marshall and Amanda are at the park flying kites decorated like a dragon, a hawk, a Ninja and a bat. They have let out 70, 85, 90 and 110 meters of kite string. Sail through these clues to determine who is flying each kite and what height each kite has reached.

Clues

1. Seth and the girl flying the hawk kite have their kites higher than the boy who is flying the dragon and the girl with the bat kite.

2. Louise's kite is higher than the dragon and the bat kite but not as high as the Ninja kite.

3. The dragon kite flies higher than the bat kite.

	dragon	hawk	Ninja	bat	110 meters	90 meters	85 meters	70 meters
Seth								
Louise								
Marshall								
Amanda								
110 meters								
90 meters								
85 meters								
70 meters								

Arbor Day

Stacey, Courtney, Evan and Gregory are planting white pine, red bud, flowering crab and oak trees for Arbor Day. They are planting 20, 4, 3 and 2 trees each. Dig into these clues to discover who is planting each kind of tree and how many they are planting.

Clues

1. Stacey will get her dad to help and together they plan on planting more than the girl planting flowering crab and the boy with oak but fewer trees than Gregory.

2. Courtney will plant fewer than Gregory and the girl planting red bud but more than the boy planting oak.

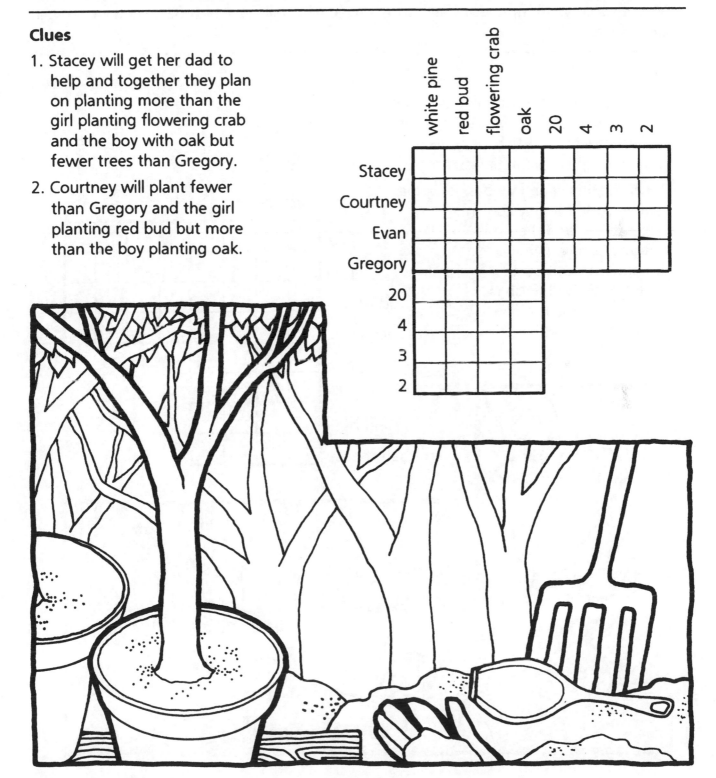

Pasta-Rama

Kyle, Latisha, Matthew, and Jacqueline are in a pasta-cooking contest. They are using fettucine, linguine, manicotti, and vermicelli in their recipes. They all have a secret ingredient (oregano, garlic, sweet basil, and grated Parmesan cheese) that they believe will ensure success. Stir up these clues to determine who will use which pasta and which secret ingredient.

Clues

1. Kyle, the girl using linguine, the boy using lots of garlic, and the girl with fresh sweet basil all have revised their recipes several times.

2. Latisha, her friend who is using the manicotti, the boy cooking vermicelli, and the boy seasoning with Parmesan cheese all think they will finish as one of the top five finalists.

	fettucine	linguine	manicotti	vermicelli	oregano	garlic	sweet basil	Parmesan cheese
Kyle								
Latisha								
Matthew								
Jacqueline								
oregano					
garlic					
sweet basil					
Parmesan cheese					

© Taylor & Francis Group · *Logic Safari, Book 2*   DOI: 10.4324/9781003236290-21

Peter and the Wolf

Lauren, Jeremy, Linsey and Robert went with their class to see a performance of *Peter and the Wolf*. Each student had a different favorite character. Their favorites were Peter, Grandfather, the wolf and the bird. Each student noticed something special about the hall that they mentioned when they wrote about their trip. They made note of the chandeliers, velvet seats, instruments and the conductor. Tune up these clues to discover who liked each character and what thing each person found fascinating.

Clues

1. Lauren, the boy who liked Peter, the girl who admired the velvet seats, and Robert all followed the teacher's instructions about getting from the bus into the hall.

2. Linsey, the boy who admired Grandfather, the boy who was impressed by the gigantic chandeliers, and the girl who got to meet the conductor were amazed at how many students attended the performance.

3. The person who enjoyed the wolf was not the person who was impressed with the velvet seats.

	Peter	Grandfather	wolf	bird	chandeliers	velvet seats	instruments	conductor
Lauren								
Jeremy								
Linsey								
Robert								
chandeliers					
velvet seats					
instruments					
conductor					

Closing the Office

Brianna, Angela, Jenny, David, Lisa and John work part-time in an office. Each is responsible for one task at closing time. Each person has to either lock the door, forward the phone to the answering service, unplug the coffee pot, turn off the copier, lock the files, or store the day's work on a computer disk. Sort through these clues to determine who has what duty.

Clues

1. Brianna, Angela, Jenny, the boy who unplugs the coffee pot, the girl who forwards the phone, and the boy who stores information on the computer all enjoy their jobs.

2. David, Lisa, John, the girl who locks the door, the girl who locks the files, and the girl who turns off the copier all share responsibilities in the office.

3. David, Angela, Jenny, the boy who stores information on the computer, and the girl who turns off the copier look forward to payday.

4. Angela does not lock the door.

	door	phone	coffee pot	copier	files	computer
Brianna						
Angela						
Jenny						
David						
Lisa						
John						

© Taylor & Francis Group • *Logic Safari, Book 2*   DOI: 10.4324/9781003236290-23

Bird Scouting

Mrs. Bishop took a group of boys on a bird scouting expedition. Each boy sighted either a killdeer, a grosbeak, a martin, a robin, a cardinal, a mockingbird, a thrasher or a blue jay. Scout through these clues to determine which boy spotted which bird.

Clues

1. Taylor, and the boy who spotted a grosbeak, and the boy who sighted the cardinal, and the boy who saw a thrasher shared a pair of binoculars.

2. Matthew, and the boy who saw the killdeer, and the boy who spotted the martin, and the boy spying a mockingbird all spotted their birds in a meadow by the woods.

3. Damon, Perry, Justin, the boy who saw a killdeer, and the boy who spotted a robin all complained of being hungry long before their lunch break.

4. Damon, Cortez, the boy who found a cardinal, the one who spotted a blue jay, and the one sighting the thrasher studied the nesting habits of their birds.

5. Justin, Ty, Dane, the boy spotting a killdeer, the boy who saw the grosbeak, the boy who spied the robin, and the boy with the blue jay are earning points for an ornithological badge.

6. Taylor, the boy who saw the killdeer, the boy who saw the martin, the boy who saw a cardinal, the boy who saw a blue jay, and Perry all collect feathers.

7. Matthew, Perry, Dane, the boy sighting the mockingbird, and the boy who spotted the grosbeak are careful to avoid disturbing bird nests.

8. Dane, Ty, and the boy who spotted a martin are building bird houses.

	killdeer	grosbeak	martin	robin	cardinal	mockingbird	thrasher	blue jay
Taylor								
Matthew								
Damon								
Perry								
Justin								
Cortez								
Ty								
Dane								

Scent Survey

Cynthia interviewed members of her family (Uncle Kent, Aunt Helen, Joyce, Ed, Aunt Shirley, Aunt Brenda, Grandma Frances, Grandma Hope, Grandpa John and Grandpa Sam) for a class project. She found that their favorite smells were freshly mown grass, lilacs, frying bacon, fresh baked bread, new car interiors, roses, a pine forest after a rain, the ocean, hyacinths and baby powder. Sniff your way through these clues to determine each person's favorite smell.

Clues

1. Joyce, Aunt Brenda and Grandma Hope all have floral favorites.

2. Uncle Kent and Grandpa Sam named food aromas as their favorites.

3. The grandfather who loves the smell of grass and the grandmother who loves lilacs are married.

4. The uncle who loves the smell of frying bacon is the brother of the aunt who loves roses.

5. The grandmother whose favorite smell is baby powder is the mother of the aunt who loves the ocean and the aunt who loves the smell of pine trees.

6. Aunt Helen is not the person who loves the smell of pine.

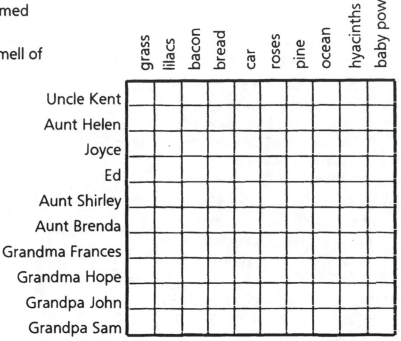

	grass	lilacs	bacon	bread	car	roses	pine	ocean	hyacinths	baby powder
Uncle Kent										
Aunt Helen										
Joyce										
Ed										
Aunt Shirley										
Aunt Brenda										
Grandma Frances										
Grandma Hope										
Grandpa John										
Grandpa Sam										

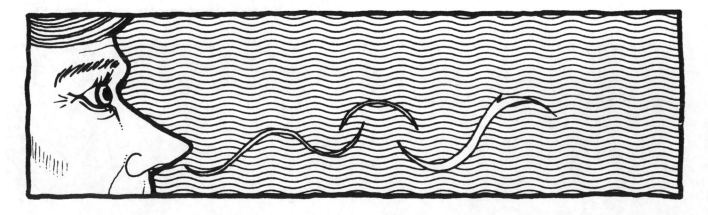

 © Taylor & Francis Group • *Logic Safari, Book 2*   DOI: 10.4324/9781003236290-25

School Directory

Ten parents have volunteered to put together the school directory. Their individual assignments are addresses, index, calendar of events, faculty directory, enrollment by class, advance sales, typing, artwork, binding and distribution. Read through these clues to find out who has what job.

Clues

1. Mrs. Rosenberg, Mrs. Schmidt, Mr. Ford, the mother working on the faculty directory, the woman in charge of advance sales, the man doing the artwork and the father who will do the binding have helped on the school directory in previous years.

2. Mrs. Ingram, Mr. Ford, Mr. Martinez, Mr. Boyer and the man working on distribution have definite deadlines.

3. Mrs. Reed, Mr. Boyer, Mrs. Adkins, Mrs. Rosenberg, Mrs. Graham, the man in charge of the artwork and the woman in charge of the calendar of events are all enlisting the help of family members.

4. Mrs. Rosenberg, Mrs. Schmidt, Mrs. Ingram, Mrs. Graham, the woman doing the index and the woman working on enrollment all have more than one child in the school.

5. Mrs. Ingram, Mrs. Adkins, the woman in charge of advance sales, the woman doing the typing and the woman working on the index are looking for faster ways to complete their tasks.

	addresses	index	calendar	faculty directory	enrollment	sales	typing	artwork	binding	distribution
Mrs. Rosenberg										
Mrs. Schmidt										
Mr. Martinez										
Mrs. Ingram										
Mr. Ford										
Mrs. Graham										
Mrs. Adkins										
Mr. Boyer										
Mrs. Reed										
Mr. Shannon										

Lightning Bugs

Cory, Doug and Preston live on Cedar Wood Drive and have house numbers 374, 376 and 378. One night they were in their yards watching lightning bugs. They called these twinkling insects either lightning bugs, fireflies or glowworms. Their parents called them back inside at 8:15, 8:30 and 8:40. Ignite these clues to determine who called these friendly insects by which name, where each boy lives, and at what time each was called inside.

Clues

1. Cory, and the boy who referred to the insects as lightning bugs, and the boy who was called in at 8:15 brought glass jars to collect their insects.

2. Doug had to come in before the boy who called the insects lightning bugs and the boy who refered to them as glowworms.

3. The boy who came in at 8:15 lives between the boy whose name for the insects is glowworms, and the boy who lives at 378 Cedar Wood Drive.

4. The boy who called the insects glowworms did not come in last.

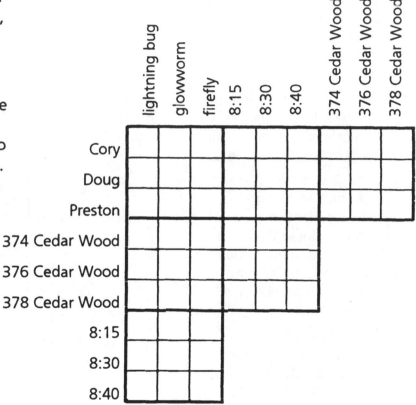

	lightning bug	glowworm	firefly	8:15	8:30	8:40	374 Cedar Wood	376 Cedar Wood	378 Cedar Wood
Cory									
Doug									
Preston									
374 Cedar Wood									
376 Cedar Wood									
378 Cedar Wood									
8:15									
8:30									
8:40									

 © Taylor & Francis Group • *Logic Safari, Book 2*   DOI: 10.4324/9781003236290-27

Mastodon State Park

Kathleen, Eric and Molly visited Mastodon State Park on a field trip with their class. Each liked something different about the museum (the movie, the fossils or the diorama). Each liked a different location on the tour (the old quarry, the new excavation and the river bluff). Each brought a sack lunch featuring either a turkey sandwich, a ham sandwich or a peanut butter sandwich. Dig through these clues to determine who liked what best.

Clues

1. Kathleen, the boy who brought a ham sandwich, and the girl who enjoyed the movie presentation were all enthralled by learning about the era when mastodons roamed that part of the world.

2. Eric, the girl who loved fossils, and the girl who found the old quarry so exciting were delighted when the ranger demonstrated how to throw a spear.

3. The girl who packed a turkey sandwich in her lunch, the boy who found the new excavation fascinating, and the girl who preferred the river bluff all knew the difference between a mastodon and a mammoth before taking the trip to the park.

	movie	fossils	diorama	quarry	excavation	river bluff	turkey	ham	peanut butter
Kathleen									
Eric									
Molly									
turkey						
ham						
peanut butter						
quarry			
excavation			
river bluff			

Summer Birthdays

Matthew, Melissa, Kevin and Kristina all have summer birthdays and are, therefore, celebrating their un-birthdays this month in Mrs. Kinney's class. Their celebrations are on the 3rd, 10th, 17th and 24th. Their mothers are sending cupcakes, cookies, ice cream bars and marshmallow rice bars for the class. The students' real birthdays are in June, July, July and August. Blow out these clues to determine who is celebrating on what day, with which treat, and in what month their real birthdays fall.

Clues

1. Matthew, the girl who is bringing cupcakes, the boy celebrating on the 24th, and the girl whose real birthday is in August are looking forward to celebrating with their classmates.

2. Melissa, the two boys who have their real birthdays in the same month, and the girl whose mom is bringing ice cream bars will all get a special prize from Mrs. Kinney.

3. Kristina will celebrate her un-birthday before the boy sharing marshmallow rice bars or Kevin but after the girl who has a June birthday.

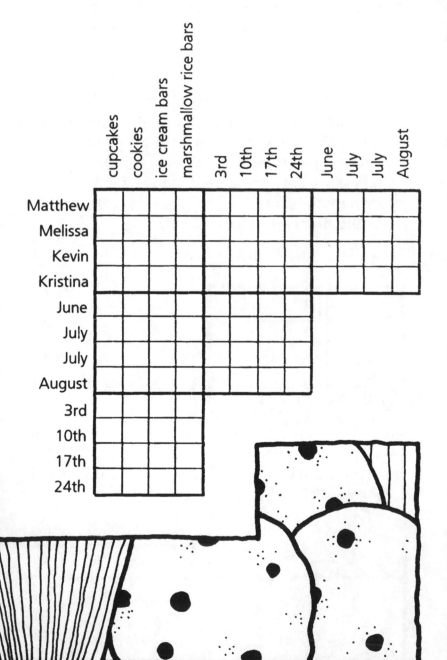

          © Taylor & Francis Group · *Logic Safari, Book 2*   **DOI: 10.4324/9781003236290-29**

Answers

1. Fantastic Gymnastics, pg. 4
Erin - trampoline
Julie - parallel bars
Megan - vault
Angela - balance beam

2. Cafeteria Choices, pg. 5
Lollie - sloppy Joe
Jay - pizza
Dominick - taco
Kristi - hot dog

3. Special Delivery, pg. 6
Sarah - bus 86, Mr. Dye
Jonathan - bus 112, Ms. Walker
Kristina - bus 54, Mr. Cipponeri

4. Lost and Found, pg. 7
Michelle - morning break, windbreaker
Jason - lunch break, ski hat
Benjamin - lunch break, purple mitten

5. Book Mark Designers, pg. 8
Shannon - rainbow, pink
Laura - pyramid, gold
Robert - garden, green

6. Coat Hooks, pg. 9
David - 16, Ms. Heath
Melinda - 8, Ms. Meyers
Cole - 14, Ms. Goodman

7. Fitness Profile, pg. 10
Grant - one-mile run, 9 years
Mary - sit-ups, 7 years
Garrett - pull-ups, 6 years

8. Class Trip, pg. 11
Kelly - museum, 6
Adam - zoo, 6
Andrea - art center, 9

9. Favorite Sports, pg. 12
Drew - football, 6
Mark - baseball, 10
Emily - swimming, 3

10. Piggy Banks, pg. 13
Marie - 45 cents, 4 coins
Vanessa - 75 cents, 3 coins
Katie - 33 cents, 5 coins

11. Can for Conservation, pg. 14
Margaret - Kindergarten, 10:45
Bradley - 2nd grade, 9:15
Tyler - 5th grade, 8:30

12. Class Quilt, pg. 15
Tommy - pine tree, paints
Catherine - musical notes, embroidery
Pamela - Big Dipper, applique

13. Student Council, pg. 16
Heather - secretary, 4th
Greg - president, 6th
Kevin - historian, 5th

14. Wind Chimes, pg. 17
Suzanne - nails, driftwood
Janet - sea shells, plastic lid
Candy - antique spoons, cedar dowel

15. Bookmobile, pg. 18
Jack - 2a, Tuesday morning
Kimberly - 2c, Tuesday afternoon
Phillip - 2b, Wednesday morning

16. Baby-Sitting, pg. 19
Kristen - Wednesday, business appointment
Dara - Friday, hockey game
Chad - Saturday, friends' anniversary

17. Turtle Race, pg. 20
Tiny Tim - strawberries, 1st
Tweedledum - pickled beets, 2nd
Pokey - lettuce, 3rd
Ferdinand - cantaloupe, 4th

18. Cloud Mirages, pg. 21
Brittany - sailing ship, curious
Tricia - sad lady, sad
Raymond - soldier, content
Samantha - winged horse, peaceful

19. Kites, pg. 23
Seth - Ninja, 110 meters
Louise - hawk, 90 meters
Marshall - dragon, 85 meters
Amanda - bat, 70 meters

20. Arbor Day, pg. 23
Stacey - red bud, 4
Courtney - flowering crab, 3
Evan - oak, 2
Gregory - white pine, 20

21. Pasta-Rama, pg. 24
Kyle - fettucine, Parmesan cheese
Latisha - linguine, oregano
Matthew - vermicelli, garlic
Jacqueline - manicotti, sweet basil

22. Peter and the Wolf, pg. 25
Lauren - wolf, conductor
Jeremy - Peter, chandeliers
Linsey - bird, velvet seats
Robert - grandfather, instruments.

23. Closing the Office, pg. 26
Brianna - copier
Angela - files
Jenny - door
David - coffee pot
Lisa - phone
John - computer

24. Bird Scouting, pg. 27
Taylor - robin
Matthew - blue jay
Damon - grosbeak
Perry - thrasher
Justin - martin
Cortez - killdeer
Ty - mockingbird
Dane - cardinal

25. Scent Survey, pg. 28
Uncle Kent - frying bacon
Aunt Helen - ocean
Joyce - hyacinths
Ed - car
Aunt Shirley - pine
Aunt Brenda - roses
Grandma Frances - baby powder
Grandma Hope - lilacs
Grandpa John - grass
Grandpa Sam - baking bread

26. School Directory, pg. 29
Mrs. Rosenberg - typing
Mrs. Schmidt - calendar
Mr. Martinez - artwork
Mrs. Ingram - faculty directory
Mr. Ford - addresses
Mrs. Graham - sales
Mrs. Adkins - enrollment
Mr. Boyer - binding
Mrs. Reed - index
Mr. Shannon - distribution

27. Lightning Bugs, pg. 30
Cory - glowworm, 374 Cedar Wood, 8:30
Doug - firefly, 376 Cedar Wood, 8:15
Preston - lightning bug, 378 Ced Wood, 8:40

28. Mastodon State Park, pg. 31
Kathleen - fossil, river bluff, pear butter
Eric - diorama, excavation, ham
Molly - movie, quarry, turkey

29. Summer Birthdays, pg. 32
Matthew - marshmallow rice ba 17th, July
Melissa - cupcakes, 3rd, June
Kevin - cookies, 24th, July
Kristina - ice cream bars, 10th, August

Common Core State Standards Alignment Sheet
Logic Safari (Book 2)

All lessons in this book align to the following standards.

Grade Level	Common Core State Standards in ELA-Literacy
Grade 3	RF.3.3 Know and apply grade-level phonics and word analysis skills in decoding words. RF.3.4 Read with sufficient accuracy and fluency to support comprehension.
Grade 4	RF.4.3 Know and apply grade-level phonics and word analysis skills in decoding words. RF.4.4 Read with sufficient accuracy and fluency to support comprehension.

Printed in the United States
by Baker & Taylor Publisher Services